Young Dick Cheney

DEDICATION

To the Constitution of the United States of America.
And to the Ativa™ DX180D Cross-Cut Shredder—
"chops up to 18 sheets in a single pass!"

AlterNet Books
77 Federal Street, 2nd Floor
San Francisco, CA 94107
www.alternet.org
books@alternet.org

Cover & text design
by Robin Terra, TERRA STUDIO
Cover illustrations by Tim Foley
Interior by Jess Morphew

Printed in the
United States of America
with 50% post-consumer
recycled material and
soy-based ink.
First printing, 2008

1 2 3 4 5 6 7 8 9 10 – 12 11 10 09 08

Young Dick Cheney
Great American

BY BRUCE KLUGER & DAVID SLAVIN

Illustrated by Tim Foley

SECURE & UNDISCLOSED BOOKS

Washington   Baghdad   Kabul   CLASSIFIED

Contents

CHAPTER ONE

A Child Is Born

I T WAS A COLD AND SNOWY NIGHT in Lincoln, Nebraska, when Young Dick Cheney slipped into the world.

Harsh winter weather was nothing new to the prairie. But the brutal blizzard that beat down on Lincoln the night of Young Dick's birth was somehow different. For one thing, it was July. And yet a certain eeriness also accompanied the sudden shift in climate. The skies darkened, the wind howled—and small birds and woodland creatures scurried frantically to higher ground.

Jedediah and Mary Todd Cheney stood inside Stall 12 of the Lincoln General Birthing Barns, shivering in the cold. They were delighted to have a son, but were startled when they gazed down at their new baby for the very first time. He was born wearing wire-rimmed glasses, black knee socks and cordovan wingtip shoes.

Still, everyone thought Young Dick was a cute, if somewhat odd-looking, baby. His face and body were round, and unlike most newborns who come into the world with wild and unruly heads of hair, Young Dick sported a silvery combover. This unusual baby-pattern baldness would stay with him for the rest of his life.

His skin was also different—not pink like other babies, but instead, a grayish blue. Adding to this peculiar hue, Young Dick was unusually plump, and the ample flaps of skin that framed his face and limbs seemed to form lines and shapes on his tiny body. At first glance, he almost appeared to be wearing a pin-striped suit.

"The boy looks like a tonic salesman from Omaha," a somewhat bemused Jedediah said at the delivery table, laying his spectacles on his wife's distended belly to take a closer look. "Yes, Mother, I do believe we've got a little city slicker here!"

Even more surprising than Young Dick's appearance was his voice. He didn't cry or squeal like other infants. Instead, he emitted a gruff grumble—a kind of growl—that started from deep within

YOUNG DICK CHENEY *GREAT AMERICAN*

3

his stomach, traveled up through his chest and finally emerged from his wide, jowly face. The veterinarian who delivered him found this adorable.

Bundling up Young Dick in the business section from that morning's newspaper, Jedediah and Mary Todd began the long journey home with their new child—walking down the straw path that led from his stable, then trudging through the deep midsummer snow that carpeted the seven-mile road that led out of town.

The moment the Cheneys stepped through their front door, the proud new parents got back to work. Mary Todd resumed her chores—finishing the wood-splitting she'd started before she went into labor, preparing the family meal, mopping up her amniotic fluid—while Jedediah placed Dick in a hickory crib that he'd carved from scraps of wood he'd found behind Clem Cullen's casket factory.

As the weary couple dug into a warm supper of possum and root stew, Young Dick lay on his back in his new cradle, staring at the ceiling, his eyes open and unblinking.

Deep within the forests that surrounded the Cheney homestead, wolves howled into the dark night sky.

CHAPTER TWO

War!

FOUR MONTHS AND ELEVEN DAYS after Young Dick's birth, Japanese bombers attacked the U.S. naval fleet at Pearl Harbor, Hawaii, marking America's entry into World War Two.

Dick stirred uneasily in his casket crib.

"I think the boy's taken ill, Mother," said Jedediah. "Maybe it's the influenza. Or colic. Or too much strained porterhouse."

Mary Todd remained silent. She sensed something else was occurring.

"I think he's fixing to talk, Jed," she replied, wiping fresh gopher bowels from her hands onto her gingham apron.

YOUNG DICK CHENEY *GREAT AMERICAN*

Mary Todd and Jedediah stood over their egg-shaped son, staring down at him. The room was silent, save the faint crackle of the family's Philco radio playing out in the slaughtering shed. As Walter Winchell waxed wearily to a woeful and worried world, Young Dick jerked his head toward his parents and, furrowing his brow, uttered his first word, then rolled over and went to sleep.

Jedediah was astonished by what he thought he'd heard.

"Did…did…did he just say 'nap,' Mother?" he asked.

"No, Jed," said Mary Todd, taking a small step backward. "I think he said *'Jap.'*"

CHAPTER THREE

See Dick Read

B Y THE TIME HE WAS TWO YEARS OLD, Young Dick was a real talker, with an impressive vocabulary that easily surpassed that of the typical toddler. He never said "Mama," "Papa" or "I love you," but he did enjoy reciting a long list of "big-boy" words, such as "conglomerate," "oligarchy" and "no comment."

Just like when he was a baby, Dick continued to speak in a gruff voice. His deep, rumbly murmurs frightened the other children, but delighted his father.

"Did you hear that, Mother?" Jedediah said with alarm one day, as Dick growled his way through his favorite poem, *The Raven*. "He sounds like a movie star!"

"Who, Gary Cooper?" replied Mary Todd, smiling.

"I was thinking Bela Lugosi, actually."

"Hush now, Jed!" Mary Todd said to her husband sharply. "He doesn't sound one bit…"

But with that, Mary Todd froze. Glancing over at Young Dick, who was now reading aloud from *The Little Golden Book of Revelations*, she let out a gasp.

"Mercy!" she exclaimed. "The boy is talking out of…*one side of his mouth*!"

Jedediah looked at Young Dick and, sure enough, his son was speaking from only the left side of his face. This distressed his mother—but not Jed.

"What a funny little piehole!" Jedediah said. "It looks like he's whispering in church. Or telling someone a deep, dark secret. Mother, I do believe this child is *unusual*."

YOUNG DICK CHENEY *GREAT AMERICAN*

He tossed a pork chop into Dick's playpen and watched with amusement as the toddler snapped it up.

Mary Todd said nothing, but an expression of worry etched her brow. As she tidied up the playthings around her young son—a tin top, a wooden car, a leather chew-toy—Young Dick happily sermonized from his Golden Book, his jaw full of meat.

"Repent, or else I will come unto thee quickly, and will fight against them with the sword of my mouth…"

CHAPTER FOUR

A Magic Moment

O NE SUNNY SPRING DAY when Dick was four years old, he was playing in his front yard with a beach ball. A gift from his parents, the inflatable sphere was painted to resemble the earth, and Young Dick took great delight in making it bounce any way he wanted it to. He also liked kicking it around.

Suddenly, the ball took a wild spin and rolled off in the direction of the driveway, coming to a stop beneath the back wheels of Mr. Cheney's '38 Packard.

Crawling beneath the car for the ball, Young Dick was startled by a sudden reflection. Just beneath the tail pipe, the sun illuminated

YOUNG DICK CHENEY *GREAT AMERICAN*

a small, sparkling black puddle, creating the most beautiful rainbow Young Dick had ever seen. He was drawn to it, like a kitten to a dish of really dark milk.

Dick slid on his belly, closer to the inky slick. He smelled it—it was sweet and inviting. He touched it—it was wet and silky. Then he tasted it.

Suddenly the cramped space beneath the Packard seemed to glow, as if lit by the heavens above. Sprawled on his stomach and breathing heavily, Young Dick swore he could hear music—just like the songs of worship he heard every Sunday at St. Agnes' Weeping Face of Christ Pentecostal Church. A tingle of excitement ran up his short, thick legs.

Tossing aside the earth ball, Young Dick slithered out from under the car and darted inside.

"Pa!" he shouted, bursting into the parlor and thrusting his hand beneath his father's face. "I found this under your car! What is it?"

Jedediah took a long look at his son's moist black finger, then smiled. "Why, that's oil, son," he said. "You know: Black gold. Texas tea." Young Dick looked confused.

"It's what makes cars run," he continued patiently. "And tractors. And aeroplanes. And machines. It's found underground, all over the earth. And people pay millions of dollars for it."

That was when Young Dick Cheney had his first heart attack.

DURING HIS WEEKLONG STAY at Lincoln Pediatric Hospital and Draft Animal Clinic, Young Dick underwent a battery of procedures that would have been hard enough on an adult, let alone a four-year-old child. At one point, he had three x-rays, two blood transfusions, five electrocardiograms and eighteen cups of hospital pudding—all in one day.

But Dick was a brave little boy, and he actually came to enjoy his treatments. He especially liked taking his pills in the medication stall, where the nurses would insert a long hose into his mouth, then blow the tablets down his throat.

"Yippee!" Dick would cough. "I'm just like Flicka!"

On the last day of Dick's hospitalization, his surgeon, Old Doc Chegley, pulled Jedediah and Mary Todd aside. He wore an expression of concern on his long, craggy face.

"I have good news and bad news," he said to the worried parents. "The good news is, your son is going home today."

Mary Todd clasped her hands to her chest and let out a sigh of relief.

"What's the bad news, Doc?" Jedediah asked.

"We need to keep an eye on him," said Dr. Chegley.

The doctor went on to explain that Young Dick had most likely been born with an abnormal heart, but that none of the tests could determine exactly *where* that heart *was*.

"It's the darndest thing," he said to the Cheneys, "but nothing shows up. The EKGs don't print out. The x-rays are all black. Heck, we couldn't even hear a beat. I mean, he's *got* to have a heart in there—he wouldn't be human if he didn't—it's just that we can't seem to find it. The nurses and I are stumped. We're calling your son 'The Boy With the Missing Heart.'"

Mr. and Mrs. Cheney were silent for a long moment. Then Mary Todd spoke.

"Will…will he be able to live a normal life?" she asked.

"I don't rightly know," Dr. Chegley replied. "But I can tell you this: Your son's one tough little man." The doctor paused a moment, then said, "He's also a *mystery*."

Back in his room, Young Dick slowly began to smile, a perfect ring of pudding circling his misshapen mouth. Behind the curtain in the next stall, a donkey brayed ominously.

CHAPTER FIVE

Bullseye!

I N DECEMBER 1946, five-year-old Dick Cheney could think of nothing else but Christmas. For months he had been dreaming about the one present he wanted more than anything else in the whole world: an Official Davy Crockett Buckaroo-Boy BB Gun, just like the one in his mother's Sears & Roebuck catalog. Whenever he spoke of the Buckaroo-Boy, his cheeks turned fiery red and his phantom heart skipped a beat. So his parents, fearing another coronary, kept the catalog away from Young Dick. But they couldn't stop him from thinking about that gun.

On Christmas morning, Dick's wish came true. Padding down the stairs in his Wendell Willkie feet-pajamas, Dick looked beneath the tree and let out his biggest and happiest grumble ever.

"Thank you, Santa Claus!" Dick yelled, grabbing the rifle and slinging it over his shoulder, just like a genuine frontiersman. "Look at me!" he shouted. "I'm Davy Crockett! Remember the Alamo!"

Young Dick gave his father a great big hug, then shot his mother in the face.

FOR THE NEXT FEW WEEKS, Young Dick never let go of his gun. He shot everything he could find. Mailboxes. Tin cans. Sides of barns. And, to his parent's dismay, other people's faces. Dick shot the milkman in the face. He shot the Woolworths clerk in the face. He even shot Pastor Thomas in the face. In church.

YOUNG DICK CHENEY *GREAT AMERICAN*

21

Dick's father came home one day to find his Aunt Enid sprawled out on the front stoop, her face pocked with buckshot, a blood-spattered fruitcake clutched in her hands. That was the last straw.

"Richard!" Mr. Cheney bellowed. "Heed your father! Come to me this instant!"

Young Dick appeared slowly from around the corner of the house, his eyes cast to the ground, dragging his beloved rifle in one hand and a neighbor's dead cat in the other.

"Richard," Jedediah asked his son, "did you shoot your Aunt Enid in the face?"

Dick was silent.

"Answer me, boy!" Mr. Cheney demanded. "Did you shoot your aunt in the face?"

Young Dick paused, then turned on his heels to walk away—but not before glancing back over his shoulder at his father.

"Frankly," he said, giving Jedediah an icy stare, "I think you're out of line with that question."

CHAPTER SIX

Go West, Young Dick!

WHEN DICK WAS SEVEN YEARS OLD, his life changed forever. The Cheney family had decided to relocate to Casper, Wyoming, where Dick's father had been offered a job with the state's Department of Agriculture as an Undersecretary of Stool Sorting. When Dick learned about the upcoming move, he was heartbroken. He took to his room in tears, refusing to come out even for supper, which was his favorite time of day.

"I don't *wanna* move. I don't *wanna* move!" Dick yelled from behind the closed bedroom door.

"But Wyoming's wonderful, Richard," said his mother, pushing open the door just enough to see the look of despair on her son's plump, gray face. "It has mountains, lakes, rivers, fresh air…"

"Who cares?" Dick barked. "It only has three electoral votes! And poor people!"

Young Dick remained in his room for an entire week, emerging only long enough to use the bathroom, eat his supper and shoot the mailman.

THE CHENEYS DID MOVE TO WYOMING after all, and Young Dick was miserable. On the long drive west in the family Packard, he stared out the window, glumly watching the vast green prairies and rugged foothills of the Rockies roll by.

"Stupid mountains," Dick muttered angrily to himself. "Stupid sky. *Stupid beauty.*"

An hour later, as the family passed through a patch of desert, everything changed. Out of nowhere, a bright silver flash exploded on the horizon, immediately catching Young Dick's eye. Pressed against the window, he could see that the peculiar burst of light was the reflection of the sun off the dome of a giant building a mile or two away.

"Stop the car!" Dick shouted to his parents, opening the door and rolling out onto the gravel before the Packard could even come to a halt. Jumping to his feet, Dick squinted at the building in the far distance, hoping against hope that he wasn't hallucinating.

He wasn't. What Dick didn't know was that his parents had decided to make a surprise 540-mile detour in an attempt to perk up their morose young son. And there it was, looming at the edge of the world—the great Los Alamos bomb-testing facility! Dick had read all about this magnificent site in *U.S. Government Atomic Energy Quarterly for Kids*, which he subscribed to.

"Happy, son?" his father asked, smiling.

"I've never been happier, Pa!" replied Dick. "Well, except for when FDR died."

YOUNG DICK CHENEY *GREAT AMERICAN*

"Then hold on to your horses," Dick's father said, hugging Mary Todd against his side, "because tonight the scientists in that very building will be testing a real live A-bomb!"

Dick could barely contain his joy. He helped his parents spread out a picnic blanket alongside the desert road, and as night fell, his excitement grew. Before long, the vast New Mexico sky turned black, and Dick could hear the countdown begin blaring from a bullhorn.

His parents stood with him, their arms draped around their son's doughy shoulders.

Then came the blast. Young Dick was mesmerized by the awesome power of his first mushroom cloud. He was enchanted by the bright green light that glowed off his parents' happy faces, and the intoxicating aroma of burning cactus. He giggled as the fallout tickled his nose, instantly vaporizing the little hairs inside. He knew in his hidden heart that somehow, at this very moment, he'd been reborn.

Wiping the fallout from his glasses and brushing back the few remaining wisps of his combover, Young Dick quietly climbed back into the Packard, knowing that nothing would ever spoil the memory of this special night. Not even the coronary that he suffered forty-five minutes later, just outside of Albuquerque.

"That bomb, that beautiful bomb," Young Dick murmured deliriously as he was being strapped to the ambulance gurney. "Wasn't it...*patriotic*?"

CHAPTER SEVEN

A Boy's Life

I T WASN'T EASY for Young Dick to move to a new state. Casper, Wyoming, in the 1940s was still a rough-and-tumble frontier town, where folks were simple, and quaint storefront businesses lined the dusty streets—from Doc Merck's Apothecary & Gun Hut to Miss Maude's Saloon & Sanitarium. The boys of Casper were tough and wild, and though Dick was able to compete with them in some activities, like pie-eating contests, his anatomically ambiguous heart kept him from matching them athletically.

While the other boys played games like "Kick the Can" and "Toss the Jew," Dick whiled away the hours at the Freemason Library and

Livery Stable, breathing in the scent of fresh manure while soaking up classics like *Johnny Tremain*, *The Adventures of Huckleberry Finn* and *Attila: The Misunderstood Hun*.

It was here among the stacks and haystacks that Young Dick met two local boys named Donny and Scooter, notorious pranksters with a reputation for clever kinds of mischief—like letting the air out of the tires of *The Casper Bugle*'s delivery truck, making crank calls to the Sheep Crisis Hotline or pouring yellow Kool-Aid into the town's water supply. (They had wanted to use the corn liquor from Farmer Boone's secret still, but it was padlocked. As Donny explained, "You spike the well with the beverage you have.")

Young Dick admired the boys' moxie, and the trio became fast friends. They even had a nickname for themselves: "The Three Horsemen of the Apocalypse." Dick, Donny and Scooter did everything together: bike-riding, fly-fishing, and secretly bugging the men's room at *The Bugle*.

But most of all, the three comrades loved to play war.

"I'm the General!" Donny would shout. "I order you to attack!"

YOUNG DICK CHENEY *GREAT AMERICAN*

31

"I'm the loyal aide!" Scooter would respond. "I'll take a bullet for my commander!"

"I'm the handsome and popular college senior," Dick would add. "I have other priorities."

Young Dick also liked to build hidden bunkers out of branches and rocks, then hide inside of them, so not even Donny and Scooter could find him.

"I call them my *secure and undisclosed locations*," Dick later explained to his pals. "They protect me in times of war. This way, if you guys get killed, I can still run things. It's what *real* leaders do—you can look it up."

One day, Young Dick was collecting materials for another one of his top-secret lairs, when he came upon Casper's famous peach tree in the Town Square, just outside Miss Molly's Hats 'n' Head Shoppe. From the moment Dick had arrived in Casper, he'd been captivated by that tree, imagining the joy of taking those beautiful, old, fruit-laden branches and making something useful out of them.

Young Dick looked around and saw that no one was watching. Stooping down, he quietly removed a small axe from his briefcase, then chopped down the tree and carried it off to his latest hideaway.

Naturally, it didn't take long for the townsfolk to begin missing their beloved tree. Doc Merck was the first to comment on the theft while getting a tooth extracted at Byrd's Blacksmith, Hoodery & Tooth Extractium.

"A peash twee doethn't dust det up and wun away," said Doc.

"I'd say it was one of them Negro boys who swiped it," responded Old Man Byrd, "'cept that we don't *have* any Negroes."

An investigation was launched, and Young Dick was soon revealed as a possible suspect in a letter to the editor of *The Bugle*. The author signed his name only as "Robert N."

"He's got the motive and he's got the means," the letter read. "And while we're on the subject, has anyone noticed the peach juice that's always running down his face? The evidence is ~~Plame~~ plain to see."

Young Dick's parents were outraged by the allegations, so Mr. Cheney decided to approach his son about it directly.

"Richard," Jedediah asked Dick, who was out on the back porch, reading up on petroleum subsidies and snacking on a peach. "Did you chop down that tree?"

Young Dick stopped chewing and lowered his head. He knew that the time had come to level with his father. Here was the man who had given him life, fed him, clothed him and supported him through two heart attacks. He deserved nothing less than the truth.

Young Dick stood up and approached his father. Swallowing hard and puffing out his chest, he looked Jedediah squarely in the eye.

"Dear Father," he said with conviction. "I cannot tell a lie. Scooter did it."

CHAPTER EIGHT

School Days

IN CASPER'S one-room elementary schoolhouse, Dick was an eager student with an active imagination. He'd frequently drift off in class, creating vivid fantasies inside his head, wild tales he found far more exciting than all the dry and useless information his teachers were forcing him to memorize—like obscure dates, longitudes and latitudes, and his least favorite subject, the Bill of Rights.

"*Bo*-ring!" Dick would say.

Even during recess, Dick would remain in the classroom filling slate after slate with his literary flights of fancy—adventures that took place in faraway lands like Persia or exotic islands like New York City.

YOUNG DICK CHENEY *GREAT AMERICAN*

36

In these places of wonder, Young Dick imagined, elaborate battles were fought between bad men in suits of armor and good men in suits and ties, and right always triumphed over wrong.

Uplifting morals often accompanied Dick's tales, as the "evildoers" would recognize the error of their ways and then welcome their conquerors as liberators. Flowers figured prominently in these yarns.

Although Dick's instructors admired his creativity, they clashed with him when he began submitting his stories as assigned history reports. One of his teachers, Mr. Blitzer, was particularly hard on Young Dick.

"You call this a history paper?" he asked one afternoon, waving Dick's paper in the air.

"It's history the way it *ought* to be," Dick replied.

"Mr. Cheney," snapped Mr. Blitzer, "the United States of America did *not* 'invade and mercilessly annihilate' Russia at the end of World War Two!"

"But we should have," argued Dick. "We would have been welcomed with flowers. Beautiful Russian flowers!"

"Be that as it may," replied Mr. Blitzer, "you *cannot* rewrite history."

Dick grabbed his paper and sank low at his desk. *Says you, Mr. Blitzer!* he thought. *You don't know much about history. Or biology. Or science books—or even the French I took!"* Dick hummed softly to himself while he pondered these words.

Mr. Blitzer subsequently gave Young Dick an F on his paper and told him he'd have to retake the class. But that wouldn't happen: The following weekend, Mr. Blitzer was killed in a freak hunting accident. The shooter was never found.

THE YEARS PASSED, and Young Dick grew accustomed to his new home state. He also grew. By the time he'd reached sixth grade, he was a husky, robust young man. Still sporting the same wire-rims he'd worn when emerging from his mother's womb, he now dressed in the clothing of the typical Wyoming youth—dungarees, a flannel shirt, and a fringed suede jacket with matching suede pocket-protector.

And on his lapel, Young Dick wore a tiny American flag that he'd won at the 4-H Club's annual Pie-Off. He never removed it.

Still, Dick secretly felt uncomfortable—and it wasn't his unusual girth that was the problem, but rather a nagging feeling that he didn't belong.

Although he loved sports, he knew he would never be an athlete, having now had two more heart attacks, the first during the greased-pig contest at the Casper County Fair (he was never caught), the second while attempting to shave his back.

But deep inside, Young Dick also had an inner sense that he was cut from a different, albeit significantly larger, cloth. When he and his friends went camping in the woods, for instance, the rest of the boys would scale the trees while Dick daydreamed about how much lumber the forest could yield. When they went whitewater rafting, he envisioned a giant hydroelectric plant shimmering on the riverbank. When they went hiking up a mountain, he pretended he was a brawny strip miner, bravely denuding everything in his path.

Like a real frontiersman, Dick knew that woodland animals could best be appreciated when their heads were mounted on a plaque.

Wildflowers were at their most glorious when gathered in the great yellow scoop of a bulldozer. And true friends were meant to be shot in the face.

Yes, Young Dick sometimes felt like he was speaking a language all his own. But one day, as he stretched out on the family davenport agonizing over a clue in that day's crossword puzzle ("World's second-largest religion," five letters, starts with ISLA-), he became hypnotized by a voice emanating from the family's small black-and-white DuMont television.

"Are you now, or have you ever been, a member of the Communist Party?" the courageous, inspiring orator demanded.

Dick jumped up, ran to the TV and stared at the screen. *That voice! That charisma! That combover!* he thought. His absentee heart stirred. Reaching for his bottle of St. Joseph's Nitroglycerin for Children, Dick remained transfixed.

In the handsome, heroic junior senator from Wisconsin, Young Dick Cheney had found his muse.

CHAPTER NINE

The Blue Suit

LIFE REMAINED HARD in Wyoming, and the Cheneys struggled to make ends meet. Food was scarce, and luxuries were out of the question.

But that didn't stop Young Dick from dreaming. One day as he was walking home from his elocution class, he passed Gabby's Horse Spa & Haberdashery and stopped dead in his tracks. There in the window, smartly draped on a display mannequin, was a spectacular sight: a dark blue suit with a white dress shirt and red tie.

Young Dick had never seen anything like it before. Everyone in town dressed like cowboys, he'd often complain, and "putting on your

Sunday best" meant wearing clothes with no manure on them. This magnificent suit was something different. Something *respectable*.

Dick stared at the precious garments, his twisted mouth agape, marveling at their sheer beauty. Finally, he mustered the courage to enter the store. As he approached the mannequin, a shaft of sunlight streamed through the window. Young Dick even thought he heard the same choral music that played beneath the family Packard years ago in Nebraska, only now in Stereophonic® sound.

Dick was so entranced that he didn't even notice the looming figure of Gabby Garnett standing over him.

"Like that suit, boy?" asked Gabby, his voice harsh and scratchy, his breath reeking of moonshine and hay.

Young Dick was taken aback. He struggled to speak, but he knew he had to measure his words carefully. Gabby was known far and wide as someone not to be trifled with, and legend had it that he'd once killed a man for attempting to return an item without a receipt.

"It's…it's the neatest thing I ever saw, sir," Dick finally stammered out of the side of his mouth.

YOUNG DICK CHENEY *GREAT AMERICAN*

43

"Wipe that drool from your face, son," Gabby said with a mucousy snarl, "or I'll cut your tongue out and feed it to a wolverine! You cain't slobber on that there *en-sem-blay*—it come all the way from St. Louie."

"I won't, sir," said Dick. "I swear on the grave of Warren G. Harding. How much is the suit?"

Gabby laughed so hard, two of his wooden teeth flew out of his mouth and landed in Young Dick's combover.

"That suit costs twenny dollars!" roared Gabby. "Where's a boy like you gonna git that kind of money?"

"I don't know, sir," Dick replied, "but I will get it, or my name isn't Richard Bruce Cheney!"

With that, Gabby froze, then keeled over cackling, spitting his entire upper plate into his pet hound's water dish. "Your middle name is *Bruce*?! Oh, Lord, if that don't beat all! I ain't never waited on a sissy-boy before! I thought your kind lived in Cheyenne! *Bruce! Haw-haw-haw! Broo-sie! Oh, Broooo-sie! Haw-haw-haw…*"

Young Dick barely heard the mockery. As he stepped over the sprawled-out store owner, he paused and glanced back at the breathtaking blue suit.

"I will have you," he said out loud, his voice barely audible above Gabby's snorts. "Nothing can stop me!"

Dick knew that the time had come for him to get a job.

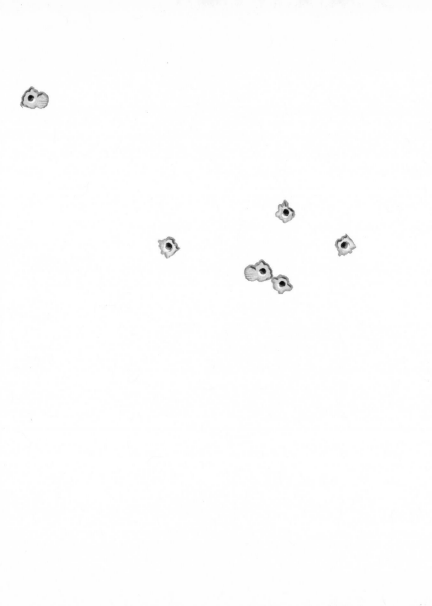

CHAPTER TEN

Dick Goes to Work

E MPLOYMENT WAS HARD to come by in 1950s Casper, and Young Dick spent many sleepless nights hidden beneath his covers, secretly poring over the Help Wanted ads by candlelight. He envied his more enterprising friends. Donny had a job with the local rabbi, "Buffalo" Bernie Mandelbaum, slaughtering kosher chickens and shipping them off to the B'nai Missoula Community Center in Montana. And Scooter made a respectable salary selling freelance items to the Town Tattler page at *The Bugle*—so many, in fact, that he often forgot the stories the moment he sold them.

But if a man wanted to make *real money*, Dick knew, there was only one place to go: the Slick Duck Oil Company.

At the time, Slick Duck was the largest employer in all of Wyoming, not to mention the state's most profitable enterprise. And Young Dick knew he was a natural for the oil business. Ever since that first time he'd come eye to eye with the magical elixir beneath his father's Packard—seeing it, touching it, tasting it—Dick had developed a gift for finding petroleum. If the wind was just right, he could even stand in his backyard and pick up the thick scent of oil blowing in from Abdul "Hootie" Az-Akim's falafel stand a mile away.

"Richard's got oil in his veins!" Jedediah used to say to folks, bragging on his son's gift. And he was serious: One night at the dinner table Dick accidentally cut his lip while lapping up the last traces of custard filling from a jagged pie tin. Instead of blood, a dark, viscous liquid seeped from the wound.

"*Mmmm*, pie!" Dick said, smiling broadly through blackened teeth, as his parents looked on in horror.

THE MORNING AFTER his encounter with Gabby Garnett, Young Dick mounted his Schwinn Black Phantom and pedaled out to Yellowstone Highway, where the Slick Duck headquarters were located. The sounds of Gabby's vicious braying still played in his head, but that only made Dick pedal harder—the wind at his back; his fiery, astigmatic eyes burning with anticipation; his thin wisps of hair flying straight up like the tines of a pitchfork.

As he made the turn onto the Slick Duck compound, Young Dick caught his first glimpse of the tumescent derricks towering against the blue Wyoming sky, their majestic rigs drilling and pumping into the soil. The sound of jackhammers against rock soon played in the background like a beautiful symphony, and the heady smell of bubbling crude began to fill Dick's nose.

The young, sweaty boy from the prairie was spellbound by it all— and promptly passed out.

When he awoke moments later, he was face down in the dirt, his bicycle lying beside him in a mangled heap. Large men wearing hardhats were pouring water over his head.

"You all right, son?" asked a burly foreman, his big, oil-slicked arms bearing colorful tattoos of dragons, skulls and Mamie Eisenhower.

"I...I...think so," replied Young Dick, slowly climbing to his feet. "What happened?"

"Looks like you were riding towards here," said the soiled foreman, "the wind at your back; your fiery, astigmatic eyes burning with anticipation; your thin wisps of hair flying straight up like the tines of a pitchfork. Then you hit the deck."

Young Dick looked at the grease-covered foreman. Taking a deep breath, he stood up, flattened his combover and confidently brushed away the pebbles that were embedded in his chins.

"I'm here to work for the Slick Duck Oil Company, sir!" he announced.

A sympathetic smile crossed the foreman's dirty, dripping face. "That's great, son," he said, "but I'm afraid you're going to have to wait a few years. Wyoming law says you have to be at least twelve before you can work on an oil rig—same age as when you can drink, get hitched and shoot yer kin. Sorry, chief."

Dick felt a familiar tightening in his chest, and he tried to respond. But by then, the malodorous foreman had turned to his crew. "Okay, boys, show's over. Let's get back to work. Remember, that prize money's still out there—twenty dollars for the first man to find a new patch of oil."

"Did...did you say twenty dollars, mister?" asked Young Dick, grabbing the foreman by his stinking, filthy sleeve.

"That's right," said the hygienically toxic man, laughing. "But like I said, you can't be a squirt and work with gushers. Now clean up the black stuff that's oozing out of that gash on your knee and head on home to your Momma. See you in a few years, kid."

Young Dick was crushed. Dropping his eyes to the ground as the fetid foreman put his men back to work, Dick felt like crying. Then he started to grow angry. After all, there was nowhere else on earth he wanted to work than in a Wyoming oil field. And yet, Wyoming— the state that he loved, the state of big skies and big hopes, the state shaped just like a saltine cracker—was taking that *away* from him.

The *government* was keeping him from realizing his destiny, Dick concluded, and as he walked his bent bicycle along the dusty road, he began to talk to himself.

"Stupid laws!" he muttered, nearly swooning as he passed the oil wells. "Some day *I'm* going to make the laws around here. And then *everybody's* going to be sorry!"

Work, Dick, Work!

THE NEXT MORNING, Dick wasn't feeling much better.

"What's the matter, Richard?" Mary Todd asked her pouting son at breakfast. "You've only eaten a pound of bacon, and you've hardly touched your moose."

"I don't want to talk about it," Dick snapped, pushing himself away from the table. "I just want to be left alone."

Grabbing his fringed suede windbreaker, he swung open the screen door and stormed out into the front yard. Then he began to walk. This was something Young Dick did when he needed to think.

Like before he took an exam at school. Or after a church sermon on Sundays. Or whenever he shot a friend in the face.

Before long, Dick found himself in a sun-dappled meadow, its deep green grass dotted with a dazzling palette of colorful wildflowers. Majestic trees swayed in the breeze, almost in rhythm to the whispering of the leaves and the lilting chirp of birds.

Young Dick glanced upward and saw great blue herons, spotted owls, and even a lone bald eagle circling overhead. Down by a pristine stream, he spotted snow-white trumpeter swans beating their giant wings and a noble male elk sipping quietly from the crystalline water. Far off, he even thought he spied a herd of buffalo lumbering over the horizon, and a king cheetah devouring a wildebeest.

Young Dick was awestruck by this untouched tract of wilderness and only wished that he had brought along his gun.

He lay down in the soft embrace of the meadow and allowed his senses to open fully to the glory around him: the sights, the sounds, the smells, the smells, the smells, the sm— Wait! *What was that wonderful smell?*

YOUNG DICK CHENEY *GREAT AMERICAN*

57

Young Dick bolted upright. Unexpectedly, the wind had shifted slightly, and a familiar aroma drifted into the meadow. Dick began to sniff the air with urgency and excitement, like a dog sniffing his favorite mate's hindquarters. Mixed in among the scent of honeysuckle and blackberry was an unmistakable smell—and Dick sprang to his feet and sprinted off to find its source.

Up the hills he clumped, around the stream, over the river and through the woods, until at last he stumbled into a hidden glen and then instantly dropped to his hands and knees. Burying his face in the soil, he inhaled deeply.

Young Dick Cheney had just found oil.

ONE WEEK LATER, Dick stood on that very same spot of land. He wore a spanking new blue suit that he'd bought from Gabby Garnett, using the Slick Duck prize money. The company had taken notice of the young petroleum prodigy, and made the boy with the golden nose their unofficial mascot. Dick had even earned himself a few special nicknames, given to him by the stench-ridden foreman and his crew—endearing monikers like "The Little Driller Boy," "Oily Dick" and "Fatso."

But none of this—not the money, not the suit, not even his fleeting moment of fame—could compare with the feeling of deep satisfaction Dick felt as he watched that beautiful meadow cleared and drilled for the very first time.

"Now it's *perfect*," Dick said softly, as a tiny black tear rolled down his cheek.

CHAPTER TWELVE

Field of Dreams

B
Y 1957, YOUNG DICK was at a crossroads in his life. He'd grown up quickly in the past few years and now felt different from the other boys and girls of Casper. Maybe even a little *better*.

His experience at the Slick Duck Oil Company had given Dick a new sense of purpose—not to mention a part-time job. Impressed with the boy wonder's knack for detecting undiscovered oil reserves, Slick Duck's site-reconnaissance chief, Field Marshal Bolton, had bent the rules and hired Dick as a Junior Ground-Sniffer, off the books. The job not only impressed Donny and Scooter, but also satisfied Dick's innermost secret: a longing to outdo his father.

I'll take Ground-Sniffer over Stool-Sorter any day, Dick would often think to himself.

Junior Ground-Sniffers were the backbone of Slick Duck, and the new recruit excelled at his job. Every morning at sunrise, a search team would load Young Dick onto the flatbed of a pickup, then cart him around the Slick Duck compound. Dick would furtively scan the horizon—snorting frantically at the air—until, suddenly, his eyes would widen and he'd hoist his hand upward, shouting for the driver to stop. Then he'd jump out of the truck, squat down and sink his head into the soil.

More often than not, Dick would withdraw his face from the earth in triumph, a telltale black streak across his nose signaling that he'd found another potential gusher. Only once, in fact, did Dick fail in his search for oil. He'd had a cold that morning, and his clogged sinuses played havoc with his nasal dexterity. Consequently, Dick plunged face-first into a fresh deposit beneath a work-field Porta-Potty™. The experience left him demoralized. And stinky.

Outside of work, Young Dick felt socially restless. Now a meaty sixteen-year-old, and a junior at Casper High School, he experienced

YOUNG DICK CHENEY *GREAT AMERICAN*

the unfamiliar stirrings of any young man who longed to impress his peers. He wore his blue suit to school every day—even in gym class—carefully hand-washing it each night in the fresh, bubbling stream behind Farmer Pellegrino's barn.

But as dapper as Dick was, he still failed to attract the kind of attention he craved. It was a longing that sprang not from his head, not from his soul, not even from his cryptic heart.

No, this hunger came from his pants.

CHAPTER THIRTEEN

A Girl Called Lynne

HER NAME WAS LYNNE ANN VINCENT. And from the moment she entered Young Dick Cheney's life, he knew that his world had changed forever.

Lynne was far from a typical Casper teenager. Born to a family descended from Mormon pioneers, she was petite and outspoken, with a winning smile and porcelain skin—made from actual porcelain by a plastic surgeon in Laramie. Indeed, Lynne was the first girl in Wyoming history to have undergone complete head-to-toe cosmetic surgery, at the age of seven.

"I'm perfect inside," she had announced to her team of dumbstruck doctors at Monsanto Memorial Hospital. "Now make the rest of me match!"

Aside from her synthetic allure, Lynne was also known for preaching prairie piety, and she barnstormed throughout Natrona County, lecturing locals about the virtues of moral righteousness. She was popular at school, too, having been elected three straight years as Casper High's "Most Morally Righteous Student."

Lynne came by her reputation naturally. Her father, Ezekiel Vincent, was a renowned local minister and proud polygamist; and (one of) her mother(s), Patience, was a part-time sheriff [1] whose hobbies included needlepoint and fan-dancing. Together, the Vincents were a fine old Casper family that embraced traditional American values, such as going to church, helping the poor and chasing Chinamen.

Lynne was the free-spirit of her family—a "tomboy" some called her—and Dick noticed this unique combination of femininity and ruggedness the first time he laid eyes on her. He was in the town

---

1. *Wikipedia*

library one Saturday, reading his favorite book, *Geological Anomalies in the Oil-Rich Regions of Lower Kyrgyzstan*. His celebrated nose was buried in the tome, and his blue suit jacket was neatly draped over the back of his chair.

Walking past Dick, Lynne abruptly stopped, glanced down at him and, for no particular reason, snatched a strap of his suspenders, yanked it back and then let go—producing a loud thwacking sound against the rubbery thickness of Dick's hide.

"Nice book, Rock Boy," she said.

Dick was smitten.

GETTING A MOMENT ALONE with Lynne, however, was not easy for the lovesick Dick, as she was always in the company of the same three girlfriends: Chris, Pat and Geoff. The foursome was famously inseparable—"joined at the hip," some said—and always engaged in activities that frontier girls loved, like lace-making and log-rolling.

YOUNG DICK CHENEY *GREAT AMERICAN*

68

Yet Lynne was equally at ease with the boys in her class, which further inflamed Dick's desire to attract her attention. Whenever he'd spot her in the hallways, or in the cafeteria, or at the next urinal, he would try to impress her by debonairly inserting his entire comb into his mouth, then slicking down his two dozen hair strands with fresh globs of saliva. He had learned this trick from his new friend, Wolfie, a transfer student from Heschel High in Helena; and since Wolfie was known to be quite the ladies man, Dick took his word as gospel. Or in this case, Talmud.

Still, Lynne was unmoved. Occasionally Dick would try to start a conversation with her, but even his job as a Junior Ground-Sniffer left her cold.

"Guess what," Dick would boast, "I can smell oil from a mile away!"

"Smell *this*," Lynne replied, demurely lifting one surgically firmed buttock from her chair, then smirking at the ensuing squeak.

Dick was resmitten.

FOR ALL HER ATTRIBUTES—her intelligence, her moral rectitude, her God-and-dermatologist-given beauty—Lynne Vincent possessed one gift that captivated Dick the most: her writing. When she wasn't running about with Chris, Pat and Geoff, she could be found in the Town Square, leaning back against the stump of a peach tree and scribbling away on a scrap of rawhide atop her Anaïs Nin lunchbox.

Most of Lynne's stories focused on the day-to-day hardships of 19th century frontier women and the infinite joys of female friendship. In tales like *Conestoga Mama, Ride That Pony* and *Wagon Ho's!* Lynne explored the many unspoken ties that bound these brave pioneer ladies together—on the prairie, on the home front, on a damp mattress in the musty smokehouse behind the log cabin while their husbands were out hunting.

Whenever Young Dick saw Lynne writing feverishly during school—her face flushed, her breath heavy, tiny beads of sweat forming on her pink, collagen-plumped upper lip—he was sure he'd found a kindred spirit. He, too, had experienced that rush of excitement whenever he wrote one of his fantasies about the toppling of a despotic dictator—and, of course, the flowers that followed.

One morning, Dick was walking to the front of his class to hand in his newest essay, *Aaron Burr: Second to None*, to Professor Hume, who'd replaced the late, bullet-riddled Mr. Blitzer. He paused for a moment at Lynne's desk and peered over her shoulder. As usual, she was scrawling madly, and Dick spied a few choice words in her text—"warm," "clammy" and "sticky." Dick smiled, recognizing yet another interest he shared with the stately coed.

"Do you like meteorology, too?" he whispered to her.

"Huh?" asked the befuddled girl, not even bothering to look up from the page.

"I said, do you like meteorology, too?" Dick repeated uneasily, an uncomfortable dampness settling onto his thighs. "I can see you're writing a report about the weather, and I've been studying that subject in Creation class!"

"It's a poem, blockhead," Lynne snapped, nonchalantly jabbing her fountain pen into Dick's leg. "But while you're here, make yourself useful: Gimme a word that rhymes with 'turgid.'"

Lynne's bluntness startled Dick and he suddenly became tongue-tied, a phenomenon made all the more difficult by the twisted shape of his mouth. Rather than continue talking to Lynne, he awkwardly limped off to hand in his paper.

Lynne barely registered that Dick had left—that is, until he was out of sight. Then slowly, she raised her eyes from her paper and took a long glance at the bespectacled boy with the navy blue suit and saliva-slicked combover. A sly smile tickled at the corners of her mouth, causing a faint hairline crack to ripple across the smooth expanse of her rosy, polymer cheek.

She liked what she saw.

CHAPTER FOURTEEN

Junior

IN THE COMING MONTHS, Young Dick continued to seek out Lynne, but her weekends were booked solid with her latest speaking tour on womanhood and morality—a series of inspiring sermons she called "Free to Be Just Like Me."

Yet even when she wasn't on her soapbox, Lynne was fiercely protected by her girlfriends, and Dick soon began to suspect that Chris, Pat and Geoff were threatened by his interest in their comely friend.

Inspired by the challenge of the chase, Dick redoubled his efforts to get Lynne to notice him. He knew he had to do something extraordinary.

At first, he thought he could impress Lynne with his nimble mind, so he entered the Quayle County Spelling Bee, surprising even himself by making it to the third round—easily breezing through words like "oleaginous," "surreptitious" and "Machiavellian." But he stumbled in the final round by misspelling the word "environmentalist."

"I'm lodging a protest," he announced into the microphone, refusing to leave the stage. "I've never heard that word before, so it must be made up!"

The judges were not swayed, and Young Dick was forcibly removed from the stage with a winch.

Yet Dick remained determined to woo the elusive Lynne, so he tried his hand at a few more hobbies—philately, numismatics, live taxidermy—before discovering that he had a knack for, of all things, puppetry. He loved manipulating his little hand-carved characters, and over time he grew skilled at pulling their strings to make them walk and talk exactly the way he wanted.

He also began collecting puppets—a clown, a pirate, a risk-management specialist—but his favorite of all was a cheerful little simpleton he named "Junior." Freckled, big-eared, and bushy-

YOUNG DICK CHENEY *GREAT AMERICAN*

headed, Junior resembled America's most beloved puppet of the time, Howdy Doody, but with a vacant stare and a cowboy hat that didn't quite fit.

But Dick adored Junior, and the lovably dim-witted marionette soon became the star player in an act that Dick was developing. However, the night before he was to debut his puppet show for the neighborhood children—and, most important, for Lynne and her girlfriends—tragedy struck: Dick was sitting on the back steps of his porch rehearsing the show's closing number, "I've Got the World on a String," when a runaway donkey from Farmer Schumer's paddock tore through Dick's yard and trampled Junior into sawdust.

Young Dick was devastated. He fell to his knees weeping.

"Junior, oh Junior!" he wailed, scooping up fragments of the puppet's shiny belt buckle. "I had such plans for us! Such wonderful plans! Damn you, donkey!"

From that day forward, Young Dick would only perform his puppet act behind closed doors, out of the spotlight, away from prying eyes—and donkeys. He grew to enjoy the seclusion.

As for Junior, Dick tearfully buried the remains of his wooden-headed friend beneath a large weeping willow at the edge of his yard, alongside a half-dozen childhood pets that he'd shot.

THE EVENING OF JUNIOR'S FUNERAL, Dick grew more despondent than he'd ever been. Now convinced that he would never capture the heart of the dazzling and cosmetically augmented Lynne Vincent, he staggered helplessly to his bedroom window.

"How can I get her to like me?" Dick screamed to the heavens. "What am I supposed to do? Invite her to dinner and watch my father sort stools? Oh, what's to become of my life? I don't want to be a Stool-Sorter!"

As it so happened, Donny was riding by on his bicycle at that very moment, making a late-night delivery of "Buffalo" Bernie's Kosher Buffalo Wings to a nearby tar-and-feathering. Upon hearing Young

Dick's cries for help, Donny stopped his bike and gazed up at his friend, who was now hanging limply over the windowsill.

"You sort with the stools you have!" shouted Donny encouragingly. "They may not be the stools you want, or even the stools you wish to have later. But they're *your* stools. Remember that."

And with a ring of his bell, Donny sped off over the hill.

You sort with the stools you have, thought a suddenly alert Dick, his friend's words echoing in his head like a thunderclap. *You sort with the stools you have!*

Seconds later, Donny reappeared at the top of the hill, his hand cupped against his cheek as he called back to his friend.

"And by the way," he shouted, "I'm running for president of the student council. Why don't you put that fancy blue suit to good use and run my campaign? Holy heck, it's better than mopin'!"

Then, as Donny disappeared once again over the hill, his final words rang out in the night air.

"And, hey, while you're at it, find me a vice pres-i-d-e-n-t...!"

Just like that, Young Dick Cheney's destiny became clear to him. He suddenly realized that he was wasting his time trying to be someone he wasn't.

"I'm not a Sniffer!" he yelled defiantly into the night. "I'm not a Scooter. I'm not a Wolfie. I'm not even a Donny. I'm a Dick! And I'm proud to be one!"

Young Dick ducked back inside and began rapidly pacing his bedroom floor.

You sort with the stools you have, he repeated to himself, over and over. Suddenly clear-headed—giddy, even—he began to take stock of the many stools in his life. His ambition. His loyalty. His puppetry skills. His ability to suck the filling out of a Twinkie in under one second.

"These are my stools!" Young Dick announced triumphantly, "and I know just how to spread them around!"

Sitting at his desk, he reached for a pencil and a fresh piece of paper, and wrote two words at the top of the page:

"Campaign '58."

Dick worked through the night. Being Donny's top adviser, he realized, would give him the perfect opportunity to make things happen from his favorite place in the world—*behind the scenes.*

As the hours ticked by, Dick toiled tirelessly. He wrote speeches for Donny. He designed posters. And he swiftly came up with a boatload of ideas on how to campaign against Donny's opponent— whoever that would be.

"I can do this," he said to himself. "And when Donny wins the presidency, we'll have the power to make real changes—like restoring decency! And protecting our freedom! And getting cinnamon buns back on the lunch menu! And as sure as my name is Richard Bru... uh, Richard Cheney, we'll be welcomed with...with...*flowers*!

"And maybe," he added with a lopsided grin, "I'll finally get a certain someone to notice me!"

CHAPTER FIFTEEN

Run, Dick, Run!

THE NEXT SIX WEEKS were a whirlwind of activity for Young Dick Cheney. He knew he had been transformed by his late-night encounter with Donny—a magical experience he privately called "My Night of 1,000 Stools." In a way, he was larger than life. In another way, he was larger than anybody in town.

Inspired by Donny's trust in him, Dick got straight to work, determined to find the best-qualified vice presidential candidate in the school. He scoured Casper High for a bright, articulate and clean young man to serve at the pleasure of the president.

Unfortunately, the halls of Casper High weren't exactly teeming with potential nominees. Scrap Cunningham, the school's popular football star, was no longer available, as he was now doing time in the county prison for attempting to fondle a pickup truck. Potsie McCoy was also off the list, explaining to Dick that he was too busy with his after-school job at Arnold's Drive-In Feed & Grain. That left only Dwayne Weed, an honors student in international affairs. Dwayne came to his meeting with Dick wearing a long white robe.

"As-Salamu Alaykum," he said as he sat down.

Dick took a pass.

Sensing that the personal interview was not the way to go, Young Dick came up with a better idea for his search. That evening after school, he jimmied open the door to Principal Reid's office and quietly began rifling through the student files in the administrator's desk. "Nothing wrong with a little private investigating," Dick whispered to himself, a small penlight clamped into his teeth on the normal side of his mouth. "After all, this is an inalienable right afforded to me by the First Amendment. Or the Fourth—I forget."

But after two hours of reviewing files, Dick came away empty-handed. It was only during his long walk home through Farmer Lu's rice paddy that the perfect solution came into his head.

"Why didn't I think of this before?" Dick said out loud, fighting off a sudden urge for General Tso's Chicken. "Donny will be so pleased!"

And the next morning, Donny *was* pleased.

"Jiminy Christmas, what a fantastic idea, Dick!" Donny announced with a hearty whoop. "Gosh, you'd make a great vice president! I can't believe I didn't think of that myself!"

"That's the point," Dick said with a low, rumbly chuckle—a sound he'd never heard himself make before. "You don't *need* to think anymore. That's *my* job."

IT DIDN'T TAKE LONG for Young Dick Cheney to realize that he was a natural politician, tackling every facet of the campaign with steely-eyed, wire-rimmed enthusiasm.

He came up with his and Donny's slogan ("We Have Nothing To Fear But People Who Aren't Like Us").

He secured endorsements from such influential student organizations as Up With Casper! (a popular pep group), Up Yours Casper! (an unpopular pep group) and The Grand Wizards of Wyoming (which, as Dick explained, was an after-school club for amateur magicians).

He even persuaded Slick Duck Oil to spring for hundreds of "I Like Donny" and "I Like Dick" buttons, though for some reason half the inventory was immediately snapped up by the school's Judy Garland Society.

Occasionally Dick would hire Scooter—who was now working nights at *The Bugle*, editing the movie listing for the Casper Calendar section—to help him research the backgrounds of his and Donny's opponents. This was a smart move for the campaign: If it weren't for Dick and Scooter's investigative savvy, students might never have found out that presidential candidate Leonard (son of "Buffalo" Bernie) Mandelbaum privately celebrated something called

YOUNG DICK CHENEY *GREAT AMERICAN*

85

Hanukkah, and that vice presidential candidate Thurgood LeCroix wasn't telling the truth when he said he was just "naturally tan."

Together, Dick and Scooter spent hours painstakingly uncovering these important biographical facts about their opponents, insisting that the kids of Casper High deserved to know the truth about their opponents.

·Needless to say, the duo's dogged investigation of the student body produced large stacks of paper. To avoid unnecessary clutter, they brought in Scooter's pet goat, Harriet, and fed the documents to her. In 1950s Wyoming, Harriet was the closest thing they could find to a paper shredder.

The boys' hard work paid off. When all the votes were counted, Donny and Dick sailed to a landslide victory—doubling Mandelbaum and LeCroix's vote tally, and tripling the actual number of students at Casper High. Young Dick humbly savored his first taste of electoral victory. He also savored most of the victory sheet cake at the election night party. Doctors would later say it was the first frosting-induced heart attack in Wyoming state history.

AFTER SPENDING A RESTFUL SUMMER in the hospital, Young Dick was rejuvenated. By the time the new school year began, he and Donny were itching to get down to business.

"We got ourselves an electoral mandate, pal," he said to Donny as they were being fitted for new menswear at Gabby's Haberdashery. "And you know what that means?"

"Gee, no," said, Donny, wincing slightly as Gabby ran a dust-caked hand along his inseam (which struck Donny as odd, considering the boys were being measured for sport coats). "What does that mean?"

"It means that we're going to make some big changes at old Casper High," Dick said confidently. "By the time we're done, that school won't know what hit it!"

Young Dick was true to his word. He and Donny immediately streamlined the student government to make it more efficient, eliminating such unnecessary offices as the student council treasurer, the student council secretary, and even the school principal.

"I'm not sure you're really allowed to do this," a sad-eyed Principal Reid said to Donny and Dick as he tied the remaining boxes of his belongings onto the rump of his pack mule. "I mean, I *am* the principal, after all."

"Not anymore," Dick and Donny sing-songed simultaneously.

And with that, the new president and vice president of the Casper High School Student Council broke into laughter and gave each other a high-five. But because it was 1958 and the high-five wouldn't be invented for several decades, the boys fumbled the maneuver and wound up slapping each other in the face.

CHAPTER SIXTEEN

Dick in Charge

YOUNG DICK'S RISE TO POWER didn't fail to draw the attention of one Lynne Vincent, who had quietly watched Dick and Donny's victory sweep with intense curiosity. Indeed, she found herself confessing a secret to Chris, Pat and Geoff.

"For the first time in my life, I have feelings for Dick," she whispered to her friends.

"Ewwww!" said the girls in unison.

Needless to say, Lynne's growing attraction to Dick made her girlfriends jealous, so she was careful to watch him from afar. She'd spend long moments lingering at the water fountain near Dick's

locker, stealing glimpses of the blue-suited junior power broker, his briefcase stuffed with directives, documents and meat loaf.

So obsessed was Lynne with Dick that she once even spied on him at work, driving her family oxen past the Slick Duck Oil Fields early one morning as he sniffed out a new meadow.

But the sight of her secret beau grunting in the mud with those big, black oil rigs pumping into the earth behind him proved too overwhelming for Lynne, and she soon grew faint.

"In and out...look at them go!" she said breathlessly. "Sniff and pump! Sniff and pump! Oh, my! Oh, my! I am *afire!*" Unable to control herself, she let out a low moan, yanked on the reins and frenziedly whipped her oxen back into town.

For his part, Young Dick was too busy to notice Lynne's blossoming interest in him, as he continued to focus all his energies on his job as vice president. In a matter of weeks, Donny and Dick had not only stripped down the school's staff, but they'd also instituted a new disciplinary system, primarily for those who were kept after school. Students with behavioral problems were no longer sent to the cafeteria after the dismissal bell, but instead were relocated to a small shack behind a drainage ditch, half a mile away.

"Yessiree, we're calling it Detention-o Bay," Donny announced to the student body during a morning assembly, as Dick slipped him index cards with the speech written on them. "But I don't want you to think of Detno as a place of punishment. Golly, no—it's a place of fairness. A hall of justice, where honor, tradition and electrodes come together!"

By and large, the students of Casper High went along happily with these new measures (except for a few dissenters, who most people regarded as "lacking school spirit" and were never seen again). As for Donny and Dick, their reputations soared—thanks in large part to Scooter, who by now had been installed as the editor of the redesigned student newspaper, *The Neo-Casperian*.

"Donny and Dick's pledge to bring honor and integrity back to student government has been fulfilled," Scooter wrote in a special front-page editorial. "This newspaper applauds you both. We can think of only two words that accurately describe your triumphs: Mission Accomplished!"

CHAPTER SEVENTEEN

A New Era

THE DISCIPLINARY CRACKDOWN at Casper High was only the beginning of Donny and Dick's reign of reform, which Donny dubbed "Operation Shock and Awesome!" For the rest of the year, the ever-smiling student council president and his ever-serious second-in-command instituted a rash of innovative policies designed to make their school the pride of Casper—and the nation.

Under Donny's rule (and Dick's direction), the boys got down to business:

The Casper High mascot was changed from Marty the Mustang to John D. Rockefeller.

It was now permissible, in some circumstances, to shoot a teacher in the face.

Shop class students were ordered to stop work on their spice racks and devote all of their energies to building Young Dick a "man-sized safe" to ensure the privacy of all student documents (under the watchful eye of the new vice president).

Even the cinnamon buns that Donny and Dick had promised during the hard-fought campaign were now on the school lunch menu, though some would complain that the rich and sticky sweets were available only to the top one percent of students.

"Gee willikers, don't you think we should reconsider that one?" Donny asked Dick in a secret meeting in a small off-campus bakery owned by Ebeneezer Dunkin'. "Some of our classmates are starting to get upset."

"Let them eat Tastykakes," Dick replied.

But for Young Dick, no administrative undertaking was as important as the senior prom. Ensuring the success of this traditional year-end event, he knew, was not only crucial to winning the hearts and minds of his classmates, but also an excellent credit to include on

YOUNG DICK CHENEY *GREAT AMERICAN*

his college applications, which he'd already begun sending out—to, among others, Sinclair Community College, Texaco Tech, and the University of Alabama at Mobil [*sic*].

In past years, the theme of the dance had been vital to its popularity with students, none more so than last year's "Cow-Pie Country Fair," with its Migrant Worker Dunking Booth and music by Howlin' Hank and the Homophobes.

But for the 1959 prom, Dick had lobbied hard for a theme that was somewhat closer to his still-unaccounted-for heart. Just two years before, his secret mentor, Senator Joseph McCarthy of Wisconsin, had died at the age of forty-eight, and Dick knew this was a chance to honor him.

"The prom will be called 'Moonlight Over the Mekong,'" Dick stonily announced at a meeting of his newly formed Secret Prom Committee Task Force. "It's got romance, it's got tropical splendor— and it will send a powerful message to our kimono-wearing friends in Red China that they can't get their chopsticks into every chunk of jungle real estate, if you know what I mean."

Dick drooled slightly when he made this declaration, sending drops of spittle flying into the air like confetti. The task force passed the resolution unanimously, not so much because they liked the idea, but because they were frightened by the wild look in Dick's eye.

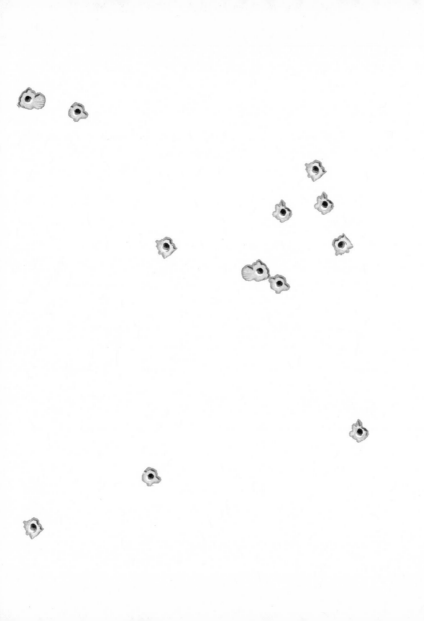

CHAPTER EIGHTEEN

The Mustang Queen

LYNNE VINCENT WAS IN A LATHER. Her sudden attraction to Young Dick had only gotten more unsettling, and now the young man with the spit-shined wingtips and squash-shaped mouth was occupying all of her waking thoughts. She even bought a stuffed elephant that she took to bed with her at night, tenderly playing with the small tuft of hair at the top of its head, fashioning it into a little pachyderm combover.

Lynne's schoolwork also suffered because of her obsession with Dick. Instead of her celebrated stories, all she could produce were lovesick tributes to her power-wielding paramour—sonnets and songs like "My Heart Goes Tick-Tick-Tick for Dick-Dick-Dick" and "Can't Help Lovin' Dat Dick o' Mine."

Worst of all, Lynne could no longer concentrate on her favorite athletic diversion: baton twirling. The reigning champion two years running at the Wyoming State Fair (and, in another event, the only girl able to thigh-crush a sack of walnuts), Lynne was known far and wide for captivating audiences with her glittery stick.

In her most famous routine, "The Wild West Inferno," Lynne dressed up as Annie Oakley, lit both ends of a baton on fire, and threw the flaming rod into the air, catching it in her peroxide-whitened teeth. Then with a mighty sweep of her head, she'd explosively spit out the flame-licked pole, flinging it into a tub of water held by her loyal Indian sidekicks, the Navajo maidens Chris and Pat, and "Big Chief" Geoff.

Ordinarily, Lynne's baton twirling was a source of pleasure for her. Now it was making her miserable: In just one day, Casper High would be holding its annual Mustang Queen Pageant, and the winner would be crowned the 1959 Prom Queen. This would entitle her to select her king for the dance.

"All I need is one super performance, Pookums," she cooed to her special stuffed friend one night in bed, "and you'll be mine, all mine!"

Lynne drifted to sleep smiling, the trunk of her plush elephant Dick clamped safely between her knees.

EVER SINCE SHE WAS LITTLE, Lynne Vincent had one overriding dream: to be Towel Girl for the Ladies Professional Golf Tour. But she also *really* wanted to be Mustang Queen. Yet the idea of doing her routine in front of her beloved Dick left Lynne in a mild state of panic. In her diary, she wrote:

Dear Diary,

Help me! In just 18 hours my life ends! How can I perform "The Inferno" with HIM there? One look at ♡♡♡♡ and I'll be a total wreck! I won't even be able to THINK straight, when all I want to do is run my fingers through those 21 hairs! (I've counted!!) To kiss that adorably crooked mouth! To loosen the buttons on that dreamy blue suit!!! (I wonder how Geoff would look in a suit! I'M SO BAD!!!) What is it about ♡♡♡♡ anyway? Is it that devilish look in his eye? Or the grumbly sound of his voice? Or is it the manly power in his arms when he's waterboarding a tardy sophomore? All I know is that I can't get ♡♡♡♡ out of my mind. The way he looks next to those big, black oil rigs—sniff and pump! Sniff and pump! Sniff and pum . . . .

NO!!! Stop it, Lynne Vincent!! Go to bed right now and never ever think of ♡♡♡♡ again!!!

xoxoxoxo, Lynne

P.S. Who am I kidding? I never thought I'd hear myself say this, but . . . I LOVE DICK!!!

Unfortunately, Lynne's condition was no better the next morning, and by the time the competition began, she was experiencing a full-blown anxiety attack. Love-starved, terrified and plagued by a small surface bubble that had erupted on the polyurethane weathercoating of her forehead, she couldn't even look at Young Dick as she walked out onto the gymnasium floor to perform.

Sitting at the piano, Miss Rice, the school's stern-faced music teacher, struck the opening chord to John Philip Sousa's *Sabre and Spurs* as Lynne nervously hurled her blazing baton high into the air. But just as the fiery wand made its slow arc, then came hurtling back down to earth, the trembling teen could take the pressure no longer. She snapped her head in the direction of the viewing stands.

"Are you happy now, Richard Cheney?" she screamed, abandoning the plummeting staff and running for the exit—along the way knocking over her Indian maidens Chris and Pat and sending the tub of water crashing to the floor.

To make matters worse, the blazing member landed on Big Chief Geoff, instantly igniting her elaborate feather headdress. Shrieking

like an air-raid siren, Geoff began darting about the gym in manic circles, further fanning the conflagration.

Dick and Donny were stunned by the spectacle (though somewhat entertained—they'd never seen a six-foot girl on fire before), and they immediately sprinted in the direction of the flaming Navajette. Knowing they'd have to act quickly, Dick and Donny grabbed the nearest object—Scooter—and threw him on top of Geoff, dousing the inferno.

But the damage had been done: Lynne's chance at becoming Mustang Queen had literally gone up in flames. As the students quickly filed out of the smoky gym, their murmurings filled the air:

"Was that supposed to happen?"

"Boy, Lynne sure was mad at Dick."

"I just got out of Detno. Can someone please help me take off this hood?"

Dick and Donny stood dumbfounded at what they had just witnessed.

"Mother of Pearl, you don't see that every day," said Donny. Then, slinging an arm around his speechless friend, he added, "I'm not a ladies' man like ol' Wolfie, but I'd say she flat-out doesn't like you."

"I guess not," replied Dick glumly.

"Jeepers, Dickie-Boy, remember—being liked isn't as important as being *respected*. Hey, I've got a meeting! Do me a favor and get somebody to clean up this mess behind me, will you, buddy? Oh, and we should probably call an ambulance for Scooter."

"Right," Dick mumbled as Donny hustled out the door.

Other than the still-smoldering Scooter, Young Dick was now alone in the gym. He found himself bombarded by a roiling sea of emotions: sadness, confusion, and an overwhelming urge to attach a car battery to a delinquent student at Detno.

Trudging sadly out of the gym, Dick suddenly noticed a familiar lunchbox lying on the floor. He glanced at the lid and knew instantly from the portrait of the lingerie-clad siren lounging on a divan that the box belonged to Lynne.

Dick picked up the small metal case and held it to his nose, hoping to get a whiff of his sweetheart. He sighed happily.

"*Mmmm*, ham," he said.

Lifting the latch to peek inside, Dick was surprised by two things: (1) there were no chips, and (2) beneath the sandwich lay a small book with the words "Dear Diary" printed on the cover.

Hmmm, Dick thought as he opened the dog-eared book. *I'd better make sure this is really Lynne's diary, so I can return it to her.* Flipping through the pages—past countless sketches of flower petals, oyster shells and Eleanor Roosevelt—he finally arrived at the last entry.

Dick read.

Dick blushed.

Dick read some more, hyperventilated, checked the general vicinity of his heart, sneaked a bite of the sandwich, read some more, and finally looked up, beaming.

Had anyone been watching him at that moment, they would have witnessed an amazing sight: Young Dick Cheney was smiling the first un-crooked smile of his life.

"She likes me!" said Dick. "She really, really *likes* me!"

"Who?" moaned Scooter, briefly emerging from a daze, then quietly slipping into a coma.

"The Mustang Queen, that's who," replied Young Dick. *The Mustang Queen.*

CHAPTER NINETEEN

A Secret Meeting

T HE ROOM WAS DARK, save the green glow of a banker's
lamp at the end of the long, polished conference table.
It was five minutes till midnight, and Young Dick Cheney
was chairing an emergency meeting of his Secret Prom Committee
Task Force. Donny was not present, having been dispatched by Dick
to a town meeting in the Rattlesnake Hills, three hours west.

"But there's no town in the Rattlesnake Hills," Donny said, as
Dick packed his overnight bag for him.

"That's why they need a meeting," Dick replied. Donny nodded
in agreement.

Gaveling the committee to order, Dick looked at the faces of the pajama-clad students assembled before him. In attendance were ████████, ████████, ████████, ████████ and ████████. Among their peers at Casper High School, they were considered the ████████ of the crop. Dick regarded them as his closest and most trusted "cronies," having shot more than half of them in the face.

Young Dick took a deep breath. He'd already counted the ballots cast by students at the previous day's Mustang Queen Pageant and, remarkably, the results were a dead heat—between Carrie O'Toole, for her interpretive dance of the Arapaho Indians' joyful relocation to northern Wyoming in 1878 (entitled "Well, We're Movin' On Up!"), and Millie Jo Stephanopoulos, the only girl in Casper pageant history to macramé her own leg hair.

"After reviewing the votes," Dick told the committee, casually setting fire to the pageant ballots and tossing them into a small wastebasket, "I regret to inform you of a voting irregularity. It appears that art student Chad Broward's unique 'horsefly ballot'

YOUNG DICK CHENEY *GREAT AMERICAN*

confused many students, and now we have, uh…a *three-way tie* for the winner.

"Therefore," Dick continued, "as Casper High School Student Council vice president—and in accordance with Rule Five, Section One of the new amendment to the Student Council Constitution, which was approved in executive session at my house earlier this evening—it is up to me to cast the tie-breaking vote. So it is this committee's *unanimous* decision that the 1959 Mustang Queen will be ██████████."

The committee members were silent.

Finally, ██████████ spoke up.

"Can we have cocoa now?"

CHAPTER TWENTY

The Big Night

I T DIDN'T JUST LOOK like the Mekong. It *was* the Mekong.

A soft blue hue filled the Casper High School gymnasium, bathing the room in a romantic mist as pinpoints of lights ricocheted off a slowly swirling papier-mâché moon. Plastic palm trees lined the walls of the gym, and smiling students strolled through a faux rice paddy that Farmer Lu had ingeniously constructed from grass, hay and three thousand little packets of duck sauce. Quaint straw huts stood at either end of the long buffet table, and at the back of the gym, two dozen freshmen were crammed into the equipment cage, costumed as imprisoned Communist guerillas. The atmosphere was enchanting.

Young Dick, dressed in a snappy new blue blazer, strode through the gym, surveying the scene with a look of pride on his face. A long line of well-wishers greeted him with warm enthusiasm.

"Great job, Dick!"

"The place looks fantastic, Mr. Vice President!"

"I finished setting up, sir. Can I take the jumper cables off my nipples now?"

Dick was proud of the work that went into "Moonlight Over the Mekong," but he was secretly worried about how the night would end. An endless stream of questions flooded his mind. *When will Lynne get here? Will she be surrounded by her friends all night? How many egg rolls can I fit into my mouth at one time?*

As he contemplated this last question at the buffet table, Young Dick heard a familiar voice behind him, looked up—and then dropped his fork.

She was beautiful. Dressed in a long green gown with a matching crown of piercing spikes—and holding a large torch in one hand and a

Bible in the other—Lynne Vincent was a breathtaking symbol of the American Dream. Shuffling in small circles around her were Chris, Pat and Geoff, dressed in traditional Vietnamese peasant garb and field hats. The inspiring tableau was a metaphorical masterstroke, as it proudly proclaimed that Lady Liberty was bestowing her gift of freedom upon peoples everywhere. With free delivery.

Lynne almost didn't attend the prom. The calamity of her pageant audition had been so humiliating that she vowed to swear off Dick forever. But after a soul-baring sleepover with her girlfriends—an evening filled with tears, truths and tickles—she knew she could no longer run away from her problems, no matter how big and balding they might be.

And so with a stiff, freshly depilatoried upper lip, Lynne came to the dance to reclaim her reputation—and, with luck, her Dick.

Realizing that Lynne hadn't yet noticed him, Young Dick swept a saliva-slicked hand across his combover, straightened his tie and sidled up to the Statuesque senior.

"Give me your tired, your poor…?" he said suavely, offering Lynne a glass of moo shu punch.

Lynne looked up and saw Young Dick. She gasped, then tried to respond—but found herself unable to speak.

"Homana, homana, homana," she stammered.

Dick smiled warmly. Only days before, he, too, might have been that nervous. But at this moment—standing in a duck sauce swamp in the Mekong Delta, chewing on a lychee nut and chatting with the Statue of Liberty—he was bursting with confidence.

"Walk with me," Dick said, tenderly taking hold of Lynne's green hand and leading her out through the school's large oak doors.

AS THEY STROLLED the Casper High campus—past the flag pole, across the baseball fields, beneath the barbed-wire fence that surrounded the Detno barracks—Dick and Lynne opened up to each other like never before. They spoke about their lives, their dreams, their least-favorite ethnic groups.

The awkwardness that Lynne had felt earlier began to lift, almost effortlessly, like the long woolen skirts of her fictional pioneer characters.

As for Dick, he soon found himself speaking to Lynne not as a friend, not as a lover, but even more intimately—like a fellow director on the board of a multinational corporation.

He spoke of one day serving his country. His tour of duty, he told Lynne, would not take place on dusty battlefields or in bug-infested jungles, but rather, in the concrete combat zones of skyscrapered America, fighting alongside the country's brave and gabardined soldiers. He spoke about someday piloting the nation from what he called "the finely upholstered back seat of power."

Lynne, too, spoke about her many dreams. She imagined one day toiling among the long and gleaming fuselages of the American aerospace industry, a job that would provide just the experience she needed to chair the government's arts and humanities councils. It was here, Lynne knew, that she could best help families everywhere to understand their values through *her* values—especially her deep and penetrating passion for womanhood.

And, of course, she told Dick, she longed to write the great American novel, filling page after page with prose that was rich, yet moist.

By this point, the love-bitten couple had all but forgotten the prom. In fact, they'd strayed so far from the school that they could barely hear the screams and explosions from the gym where, as the evening's entertainment, the football team was snuffing out a staged coup d'état by the freshman rebel insurgency beneath the papier-mâché Mekong moon.

But out in the night air, the lunar lamp that hung above Dick and Lynne promised only mystery and magic.

"See that moon?" Dick said to Lynne, pointing to the sky as he spread a blanket over a bed of nails on Detno's Field of Corrections. "We're going to put a man up there some day. And mark my words, we'll make amazing discoveries—things that will make life better for mankind."

Dick paused for a moment, imagining himself the hero of that historic first—climbing down the ladder of a spaceship, planting a

YOUNG DICK CHENEY *GREAT AMERICAN*

119

flag in the lunar soil, then planting his face beneath it in search of oil. Instinctively, he began to make a sniffing noise.

"And you know what?" he continued, "Moon oil will be just one of the many wonderful things we'll share one day, Lynne Vincent. Only by then, I'm sort of hoping you won't be called Lynne *Vincent* anymore."

Jade tears were now streaming down Lynne's face. She looked deeply into Dick's eyes, tilting her head slightly to locate them behind the thin sheen of steam that had fogged his glasses. Then she brought her face closer to his. At last, her lips softly touched down on the newly straightened landing strip of his mouth.

As the two kissed, Dick swore he heard fireworks, then quickly realized that it was just the sound of a percussion grenade demolishing the school's science room. He smiled and kissed Lynne again.

"You can put your trust in me," he whispered. "You can put your faith in me. And Lynne…"

"Yes, Dick?" she said, practically cooing.

"You can put your arm down now."

He gently removed the torch from her hand.

"By the way," Dick said with a soft smile, "have I told you how much I love your outfit yet?"

"Thanks," Lynne said girlishly. "I was hoping to include a pedestal, but—"

"You've always been on a pedestal with me," Dick interrupted.

Lynne blushed beneath her smooth coat of olive paint, creating a deep chocolatey complexion that briefly reminded Dick of heavyweight champion Floyd Patterson.

"And I love your blue blazer," Lynne replied.

Dick smiled mischievously. "Think it looks better on me than it would on Geoff?"

"What?" asked the puzzled girl. "I don't understand…"

Dick pulled away and, with a self-satisfied flourish, whipped Lynne's diary from his jacket pocket.

"I think this belongs to you," he said.

"My diary!" squealed Lynne. "But, how did you…?"

It was at that very moment that Lynne realized Dick had read her diary—and, more important, that he now knew how she truly felt about him. *It's not a big secret anymore!* Lynne thought. *I no longer need to hide it! I can finally show Dick the real me!*

And with that, she punched him in the face.

"How dare you look at someone else's diary!" she bellowed. "That was top secret stuff!"

Dick lay on the ground, flattened. So forceful was Lynne's haymaker that it not only produced a geyser of blood from between Dick's teeth, but instantly returned his mouth to its formerly lopsided shape—forever.

Lynne cocked her arm back to hit him again, but an odd sound in the distance stopped her cold. She listened carefully and heard it once more. It was the sound of screaming—*joyful* screaming—and it was coming from inside the school gymnasium.

Leaving the lifeless Dick behind, Lynne began sprinting back toward the school, following the loud, steady drumbeat of the students' rhythmic chant.

Lynne couldn't be sure, but it almost sounded like they were calling her name.

"LYNNE! LYNNE! LYNNE!"

Lynne stood at the entrance of the school gymnasium, dumbfounded. It was true—they *had* been shouting her name. As soon as she had opened the door, the deafening roar turned into cheers. *But why?* Lynne thought. *What did I do?*

Amid the clamor, she saw a grass-skirted Donny standing on the bamboo stage, holding a microphone and exhorting the frenzied crowd. Then he spotted Lynne.

"Jumpin' Jehosaphat, it's about time!" screamed Donny. "Ladies and gentlemen, here she is! Your 1959 Mustang Queen... *Lynne Vincent!*"

The students erupted into another thundering ovation.

Lynne was speechless. *Mustang Queen!* she thought, replaying her disastrous baton routine in her head. *But I was awful! I set my best friend on fire and nearly burned down the school! Who could have voted for me? Who* would *have voted for me? There must be some kind of mistake…*

She paused.

Unless…

Lynne spun around and looked behind her. Standing in the doorway to the gym was Young Dick Cheney, a small stream of black blood trickling out of his trademark crooked mouth, yet smiling the most self-satisfied quasi-smile Lynne Vincent had ever seen.

"But…but *how?*" Lynne mouthed to Dick, unable to compete with the surrounding din.

Dick walked over to Lynne. Gently taking her by the shoulders, he pulled her close to him and whispered in her emerald ear.

"Let's just say I pulled a few strings."

CHAPTER TWENTY-ONE

Long Live the King!

I T GOES WITHOUT SAYING that every queen needs a king (with the possible exception of Lynne's idol, Catherine the Great), so, of course, when it came time for the newly appointed Mustang Queen of Casper High School to choose her prom king, Lynne thrust her torch into the air and triumphantly called the name *Richard Cheney*!

The crowd unleashed a roar of approval and celebrated the coronation of their portly potentate by hoisting Dick onto their shoulders—a noisy spectacle made all the more clamorous by the symphonic cracking of various vertebrae.

YOUNG DICK CHENEY *GREAT AMERICAN*

126

When at long last the freshly crowned couple from Casper, Wyoming, made their way to the stage through the slowly parting crowd, Young Dick looked over the smiling faces in this vast sea of humanity. He saw reflected in them the long and thrilling journey he'd made from that casket crib back on the Nebraska prairie. Everyone was there.

He saw his classmates, friends and confidants, including ████████, ████████, ████████, ████████ and ████████—without whom this magical evening would not have been possible.

He saw Chris, Pat and Geoff, who despite the pageantry swirling around them continued to shuffle dutifully in tight Vietnamese peasant circles around the empty spot where their torch-bearing girlfriend had once stood.

He saw his Casper High teachers, some of whom loudly bragged to one another about being Young Dick's true mentor, while others wore black armbands and silently held up memorial photos of the late Mr. Blitzer.

He saw the townsfolk and businessmen of Casper—from "Hootie" Az-Akim, who had made a commemorative bust of Dick's head out of baba ghanoush, to Old Man Byrd, who cautiously scanned the gymnasium for uninvited Negroes.

He saw Farmers Schumer, Pellegrino and Lu, who linked arms with the rancher (and part-time haberdasher) Gabby Garnett, proving once and for all that the farmer and the cowman could be friends.

He saw Harriet the goat, bobbing her head in approval, as she happily munched on a small stack of prom expense receipts.

He saw his colleagues from the Slick Duck reconnaissance team, their bright white teeth shining like diamonds against their blackened faces, along with their filthy foreman, who with a knowing grin of satisfaction stuffed a fat envelope of "congratulatory messages" into the new king's breast pocket.

He saw the countless teams of doctors, nurses and ambulance attendants who'd brought him back from the brink of heart failure so many times over the years, now occupying an entire section of the gym bleachers and waving to Dick with one hand while holding portable defibrillators in the other.

He saw all of the men, women, children and pets he'd ever shot in the face throughout his life—some still embedded with little bits of souvenir pellets, like tiny badges of honor; others comparing their scars with pride—alongside his own Aunt Enid, who continued to clutch her decade-old, blood-spattered fruitcake.

And, yes, Young Dick saw his parents, leaning over the rope line and beaming with wistful pride at their accomplished son. Mary Todd thought back to the little, egg-shaped, spare-haired, wire-rimmed child she had spewed forth into the world those many years ago, and she marveled at the big, egg-shaped, spare-haired, wire-rimmed young man he had become. As she wiped a tear away, Jedediah stood next to her shaking his head and laughing.

"That boy is going straight to the top, Mother," Jed remarked, "and all I can say is, *'Look out, world!'*"

Out of the corner of his eye, Young Dick even thought he saw the ghost of his beloved puppet, Junior, smiling down at him. The little wooden marionette had a dim but peaceful grin on his face, as if he were saying to Dick, "I'll be right here."

Just before he and Lynne reached the stage, Dick spotted his two best friends, Donny and Scooter. The Three Horsemen of the Apocalypse smiled knowingly at one another as they recalled the glorious days and nights of their youth—the endless war games, the playful wiretaps, the fun-filled "all-nighters" at Detno. They nodded quietly to one another, then shared a manly quarter-embrace.

As Dick finally ascended to the stage, he noticed Wolfie standing at the bottom of the steps.

"Looks like you've got her right where you want her, Romeo," said Wolfie, gesturing to Lynne with a sly wink.

"Big time, buddy," replied Dick.

After the crowns were placed on their heads, the king and queen of Casper High School swept onto the dance floor for the first of many waltzes of the evening. The crowd formed a closed circle around Dick and Lynne and gazed upon them in glassy-eyed wonder.

Scooter, who was covering the event for *The Neo-Casperian*, pulled Donny aside for an official interview. Toward the end, he couldn't resist a moment of boyish curiosity.

"They look pretty romantic," he said, as the two friends watched Dick and Lynne float about the dance floor in a tight embrace. "Off the record, do you think our old pal might have his way with Miss Liberty tonight?"

Donny just laughed.

"Between you and me," Donny said, delivering an impish elbow to Scooter's ribs, "I think Young Dick Cheney will be having his way with Miss Liberty for a long, long time."

Young Dick Cheney, Part Two:
Mr. Cheney Waddles to Washington

Young Dick Cheney, Part Three:
A Storm in the Desert

Young Dick Cheney, Part Four:
Hooray for Halliburton!

Young Dick Cheney, Part Five:
From Guantánamo to Glory

MORE BOOKS FROM
THE I CAN READ HISTORY! LIBRARY:

A is for Abu Ghraib:
My First Alphabet Book!

Green Eggs and Yellowcake Uranium

Encyclopedia Brownie
and the Case of the Missing Levee

Curious George W. Gets a D.U.I.
Curious George W. Gets an Oil Company
Curious George W. Gets a Baseball Team
Curious George W. Gets Elected (Sort of)
Curious George W. Gets In Over His Head
Curious George W. Gets Really Bad Poll Numbers
Curious George W. Gets a Gold Watch
Curious George W. Gets an Old Itch
Curious George W. Gets Hammered
Curious George W. Gets a Sponsor
Curious George W. Gets a Book Deal
Curious George W. Gets a Library

BRUCE KLUGER & DAVID SLAVIN
(Authors)

Bruce Kluger and David Slavin began writing and producing satire for National Public Radio's *All Things Considered* in 2002. Their cultural and political commentary has appeared in countless publications across the country, including *The Los Angeles Times*, *The New York Times*, *The Chicago Tribune* and dozens of newspapers in the Los Angeles Times-Washington Post News Service. Their work is also featured prominently on the Internet, on such popular sites as The Huffington Post, where they are invited bloggers, and Salon.com, which published their acclaimed "Memo to George" series. Both are married, both have two daughters and both live in New York City. *Young Dick Cheney: Great American* is their first book.

TIM FOLEY
(Illustrator)

Tim Foley's work is regularly featured in magazines and newspapers across the country and around the world. His illustrations have appeared in financial publications such as *The Wall Street Journal* and *Barron's*, as well as in the children's magazines *Cricket* and *Highlights*. He lives and works covertly in the Republican stronghold of West Michigan.